Mould: The Invisible Menace

What is mould, how does it affect your health, and what can you do about it?

SARA DAVENPORT

SARA DAVENPORT

Copyright © 2018 Sara Davenport

All rights reserved.

ISBN-13: 9781983096211

CONTENTS

1	Mould can make you very ill	Pg 7
2	What is Mould?	Pg 9
3	Might you have a Mould Problem?	Pg 10
4	Mould Symptom Check	Pg 11
5	Mould Tests	Pg 12
6	Mould and Mycotoxins Types	Pg 16
7	Mould in your Home	Pg 20
8	Mould in your Body	Pg 26
9	Mould in the Foods you Eat	Pg 34
10	References	Pg 36

ABOUT THIS BOOK

This book is an attempt to make the available information on mould simple and accessible to you as a first reference. There is a list of sources at the end of this book from whom I have taken much of my text. Many of the authors have spent years investigating this topic in depth and it is to them that we should be grateful for the knowledge and techniques outlined here. If you have a mould-related health problem, please make sure they are an essential part of your reading list.

1. MOULD CAN MAKE YOU VERY ILL

Are you always tired? Do you have unexplained aches and pains that just won't go away? Do you suffer from fibromyalgia, or chronic fatigue? Breathing problems, coughs, wheezing and allergies? Asthma? Brain Fog? Is your memory no longer as sharp as it used to be? Do you get those momentary brain 'blanks' and are you more anxious or depressed than ever before?

Maybe you have been to the doctor repeatedly; searching for a diagnosis and a cure, only to be told that the tests show nothing in particular. Maybe you have simply given up, resigning yourself to the probability that you will always feel this way.

Have you ever considered that your problem might be mould?

Mould is the often invisible, unconsidered menace that can undermine your health in myriad ways. It is frequently not on your doctors list of possible triggers for illness and it doesn't show up in blood tests. Very few people think of mould as a threat, yet it is one of the most dangerous toxins you can be exposed to, and, according to estimates by the World Health Organisation[1], dampness and mould are estimated to affect 10-50% of homes in Europe, North America, Australia, India and Japan. In the US, the figures are particularly high, at approximately 50 - 80%[2]

Where there is water – and there are water pipes running through our homes that often leak without our knowledge – there is likely to be mould. Live in a rainy land and your chance of encountering mould is high. Heavy flooding will create an environment where mould can proliferate.

In the States mould is recognised as a serious contributor to ill health and it is estimated that 21% of the cases of asthma in the US may be linked to dampness and mould found in houses[3]. The American mould expert, Dr Ritchie Shoemaker, estimates that 28% of the US population has a

[1] WHO guidelines on indoor air quality: dampness and mould

[2] Mudarri and Fisk 2007

[3] Mudarri, Fisk 2007

genetic weakness to mould, making them still more susceptible to its effects. It has also been established that it is possible to suffer DNA damage from prolonged contact with mould.

If you live elsewhere in the world, however, your doctor may not be aware of the damage that mould can cause to your health, or of the fact that it can impact every tissue in your body with devastating effect.

This book is an attempt, based on the work and research of a multitude of scientists and mould experts (listed at the back), to present you with a basic introduction to mould, and give you the tools to heal yourself.

2. WHAT IS MOULD?

Mould comes in all shapes and sizes. It can be smooth and slimy, or raised and lumpy, and even covered in tiny hairs. It comes in shades of white or blue; yellow, orange or green. There are thousands of mould variations, springing up everywhere in different lands, and at different temperatures around the world. Most are harmless, but the mould that most of us recognise is the black mould, a toxic variety that causes many health problems.

Do you have it in your home? Those dark patches of greenish black that appear behind the clothes washing machine or where damp has seeped in through the walls? It thrives behind wallpaper, under your carpet or behind your old kitchen units.

Mould loves damp houses, and most grow best in a temperature of between 10-35 degrees C. It thrives on lack of light and air, damp conditions and an environment that provides it with 'food' – plasterboard, dust, wood – anything with cellulose. It needs a combination of these factors to survive and multiply, but the key to understanding mould and successfully getting rid of it, is to understand that if you remove just one of them – game over. It simply can't continue to grow.

Different mould species can have varying effects and none of them are beneficial for your health. Excessive mould growth needs to be taken care of, regardless of the species. It can lead to increased allergies and toxicity, not to mention structural problems in your home.

But it is not the mould that you see that is the actual problem for your health, it's the spores inside the mould that trigger the toxic response. These spores, or mycotoxins, spread invisibly through the air whenever they are disturbed, creating havoc and trailing health problems in their wake.

3. MIGHT YOU HAVE A MOULD PROBLEM?

Do you live in an old house? Old houses are often damp, and have airless attics and cellars where mould proliferates.

Is there a musty, mildew smell anywhere in it? Sometimes you can clearly see mould growing, but mainly it is invisible and more often than not you can't. But you can usually smell it. Mildew is an easily identifiable odour.

Have you had any leaks or floods? Mould flourishes anywhere there is water and where there are water pipes, there are often slow drips to provide a perfect mould breeding ground.

Do you have an air conditioning unit? In your house or at work? The moisture in the systems can trigger mould growth that is then spread throughout by the vented cold air.

Do you have plasterboard or drywall in your home? Or at the office or at school? Combine damp with plasterboard and you create a feast for mould to flourish.

4. MOULD SYMPTOM CHECK

"There are many mould exposure symptoms, because the illness affects multiple systems in the body, which in turn, causes the patient to exhibit multiple symptoms.'
Dr Ritchie Shoemaker

Make a list of any health issues that are currently affecting you. If you go away on holiday and feel considerably better while you are away, only for the symptoms to return when you come home again, pinpoint exactly what symptoms have flared up. Grade their discomfort on a scale of 1-10. If you have several of the following symptoms, and nothing you have done so far clears them up, then 'think mould'.

- Exhaustion
- Muscle aches and joint pain
- Kidney and bladder discomfort
- Blurred vision and sensitivity to light
- Headaches
- Stiffness
- Breathing problems
- Red or itching eyes
- Continual cough
- Frequent sneezing
- Memory issues
- Difficulty concentrating
- Forgetting words
- Mind blanks
- Confusion
- Continual thirst
- Metallic taste in the mouth
- Mood swings
- Feeling weak
- Sinus problems
- Vertigo
- Numbness
- Feeling too hot or too cold
- Tremors

5. MOULD TESTS: HOW TO CHECK IF YOU ARE AFFECTED?

1 Visit VCSTest.com
The Visual Contrast Sensitivity Test was developed by Ken Hudnall from the environmental agency of the USA. It measures how well you see details and contrast and a poor result may indicate problems with your neurons and brain function. The VCS test will show you a series of images of decreasing contrast and then record any contrast levels where you can – or cannot – identify specific patterns, shapes, or objects. In a person affected by mould, which damages the nerve cells, there will be a reduction in contrast vision. This can be managed and reversed, however, when the mould toxins are removed with cholestyramine (see Chapter 8). Regular monitoring with the test will tell you when you are clear of the infection.

2 Irlen Test
Check out www.irlen.com and take their light sensitivity test. When you are affected by mould, you tend to become extra sensitive to light and sound. Irlen make coloured lenses that resolve any problem.

3 ERMI Testing
An ERMI test will analyse the dust in your home to identify the quantity and different types of the moulds present. ERMI stands for the Environmental Relative Moldiness Index and is an objective, standardized DNA based method of testing that looks at thirty-six species.

4 Brain Scans
Dr Daniel Amen of the Amen Clinics in the USA uses the SPECT scan to check how well your brain is functioning, identifying the areas that are working well; the areas that are low in activity and those that are overly high in activity. Mould exposure causes the brain to work too hard, and then over time to shrivel.

5 Mould Markers - Blood Tests
You can tell a lot from checking certain readings from your blood. RealtimeLab.com offers a test of serum antibodies to moulds and mycotoxins.

- **Cytokine levels** – These will be high if you are affected by mould. It increases levels, triggering chronic inflammation response syndrome (CIRS); Mould can set off certain auto-immune diseases such as rheumatism and lupus.

- **Leptin** controls your eating behaviour. Low leptin affects melatonin, creating problems with managing to sleep long or deeply. Leptin levels, however, are always high where there is a mould problem because mould creates leptin resistance, an inflammatory response where your leptin levels are high but not working, triggering chronic exhaustion, pain and weight gain.

- **MSH (alpha- melanocyte stimulating hormone)** – Mould decreases MSH levels by blocking the leptin receptors in your hypothalamus, which then stops producing MSH. 95% of all mould patients have a problem with low MSH. MSH is a hormone that counteracts inflammation, regulates hormone production and defends against invading virus and bacteria. It takes longer to recover from disease without it, so is a vital issue to treat. Low MSH means reduced numbers of white blood cells, reduced sex hormones and low cortisol, which can trigger depression. Exhaustion, mood swings and pain are other symptoms. Low levels also affect the pituitary gland.

- **AGA (Anti-gliadin antibodies (IgA/IgG))** – If your MSH is low, indicating a fungal problem, then your AGA levels will be high. Anti-gliadin (AGA) antibodies are produced in response to gliadin, a small protein that is part of gluten, found in wheat, barley and rye. Within 30 minutes of eating gliadin, for those with anti-gliadin antibodies, there will be an inflammatory response.

- **VIP – (Vasoactive Intestinal Polypeptide)** – If you have mould problems, you will have low VIP levels. VIP is a neuro-regulatory hormone with receptors in the hypothalamus. It regulates peripheral cytokine responses, pulmonary artery pressures and, like MSH, inflammatory responses throughout the body. Symptoms include shortness of breath, especially whilst exercising.
VIP seems to induce smooth muscle relaxation (lower oesophageal sphincter, stomach, gallbladder), stimulate secretion of water into pancreatic juice and bile, and cause inhibition of gastric acid secretion and absorption from the intestinal lumen, which can lead to chronic, watery diarrhoea.

When VIP levels are boosted, according to a strictly administered protocol, chronically exhausted patients are restored to normal energy levels. (Do not use VIP if you are exposed to mould (with ERMI values greater than 2); if you fail a VCS test; or if you have a MARCoNS (Multiple Antibiotic Resistant Coagulase Negative Staphylococci) present in your nose).

- **MBP (myelin basic protein antibodies)** is elevated in fungal diseases.

- **TGF Beta-1 - Transforming Growth Factor Beta-1** – TGF Beta-1 is a protein that helps control the growth, division and death of cells. It plays a part in foetal development, and the formation of blood vessels, muscle tissue and body fat. It helps with wound healing and the correct functioning of the immune system. Exposure to mould and water damaged buildings can raise TGF Beta-1 levels, triggering asthma attacks, weakening breathing systems and creating autoimmune and neurological problems.[4]

- **C4a** is an inflammatory marker. Rapid rise of levels in the blood show up within 12 hours of exposure to mould and biotoxins, and levels remain high until therapy is started to reduce them.

- **HLA DR – (Human Leukocyte Antigens (HLAs))** are found on the surface of nearly every cell in the human body. They help the immune system tell the difference between body tissue and foreign substances. Dr Ritchie Shoemaker has established that almost a quarter of the normal population is genetically susceptible to chronic mould illness. Three quarters are not.

- **ACTH/Cortisol** – ACTH is a hormone released from the anterior pituitary gland in the brain. Cortisol is a steroid hormone produced by the adrenal cortex, which is the outer part of the adrenal glands located on top of both kidneys. As MSH begins to fall, ACTH rises.

- **VEGF (Vascular endothelial growth factor).** VEGF is a polypeptide made by cells that stimulates new blood vessel formation and increases blood flow in the capillaries. Mould lowers levels of

---

[4] http://www.survivingmold.com/mold-symptoms/what-is-a-water-damaged-building

VEGF, slowing blood flow and starving cells of strength and energy.

- **ACLA IgA/IgG/IgM (Anti-cardiolipins)** – Antibodies are proteins in the blood that the body produces to fight off foreign invaders, creating immunity against unfamiliar microorganisms. ACLA are autoantibodies - antibodies that instead attack your own body. They interfere with the normal function of blood vessels and react with proteins in the blood that are bound to phospholipid, a type of fat molecule that is a part of the normal cell membrane. IgA, IgM, and IgG are autoantibodies often identified in diseases such as lupus and scleroderma.
An increased risk of spontaneous foetal loss in the first trimester of pregnancy is often seen in women who have these autoantibodies. They are found in over 33% of children with bio-toxin associated illnesses.

- **ADH (Antidiuretic hormone or vasopressin/Osmolality)** – ADH is a substance produced naturally by the hypothalamus and released by the pituitary gland. The hormone controls the amount of water your body removes. Osmolality is a test that measures the concentration of all chemical particles found in the fluid part of the blood.
Symptoms associated with poorly functioning ADH include dehydration, frequent urination; excessive thirst and sensitivity to static electrical shocks, as well as oedema and rapid weight gain.

- **MMP-9 (Matrix metallopeptidase 9)** – MMP-9 is an enzyme that in humans, is encoded by the MMP9 gene. It delivers inflammatory elements of blood that affect the brain, lungs, muscles, nerves and joints and is involved with embryonic development and reproduction and associated with destruction of lung elastin, rheumatoid arthritis, astherosclerosis, cardiomyopathy and abdominal aortic aneurysm.

- **CRP (C-Reactive Protein)** – Mould can elevate your CRP levels. Yeast makes bread rise – fungus can do the same to you. High levels may indicate a mould problem.

6. MOULD AND MYCOTOXINS TYPES

Which ones are affecting you? These are the moulds that may show up on a mould test:

Aspergillus spp
Aspergillus is an 'umbrella' term for a genus of fungi that covers more than 160 different species of mould. Sixteen of these have been proven to cause serious health issues. Aspergillosis is now the second most common fungal infection requiring hospitalization in the United States.

Aspergillus fumigatus. The number one trigger for mould infection. Found in decomposing organic material, such as self-heating compost piles, it grows and flourishes at temperatures up to 55C. People who work with contaminated material often develop hypersensitivity to the spores of Aspergillus and may suffer severe allergic reactions upon exposure.

Aspergillus flavus. The second most frequently found infector. It produces the mycotoxin aflatoxin, highly dangerous and a toxic cancer causing mould. Most countries have established danger levels for aflatoxin in food, though none at all are in place for airborne exposure risks.

Aspergillus niger. The third most dangerous Aspergillus fungi, which can grow almost anywhere. It can develop as a 'fungal ball' deep in the lungs, which it manages without invading the lung tissue.

Stachybotrys chartarum (atra). This is the black mould most of us are familiar with. It grows on water damaged, cellulose-rich building materials, feeding on plasterboard, paper, ceiling tiles, insulation backing and wallpaper. It multiplies rapidly where there has been unnoticed water damage and is usually black and slimy in appearance.

It produces mycotoxins, the invisible spores contained within the mould that are extremely toxic, suppressing the immune system and capable of triggering cancer. Touch the mould, breathe it in, or eat it in polluted foods – peanuts and coffee are major culprits - and you can rapidly be in trouble. Symptoms of exposure include dermatitis, cough, rhinitis, nose bleeds, cold and flu-like symptoms. Headache? Feeling generally unwell? Fever or skin rash? Think mould.

Cladosporium spp. These are the moulds that are dark greenish/black in the front, and black on the reverse, with a powdery, velvety texture. You find them on decaying plants, woody bushes, food, straw, soil, paint, textiles, and the surface of fiberglass duct liner in the interior of supply ducts.

There are over 30 species in the Cladosporium genus. The most common are C. elatum, C. herbarum, C. sphaerospermum, and C. cladosporioides. They can trigger skin lesions, keratitis, nail fungus, sinusitis, asthma, and pulmonary infections. Extreme exposure can lead to oedema and bronchiospasms, and long term, to pulmonary emphysema.

Fusarium spp. This is often found in humidifiers and water-damaged carpets and is considered one of the most poisonous of the moulds. Fusarium spp. are frequently involved with eye, skin, and nail infections. You can breathe it in, or get infected through eating contaminated grains. It triggers eye, skin and nail infections with side effects including nausea, vomiting, diarrhoea, dermatitis and extensive internal bleeding.

Several species can produce the trichothecene toxins which target the circulatory, alimentary, skin, and nervous systems. Vomitoxin, the aptly named mycotoxin, has been associated with outbreaks of acute gastrointestinal upsets. Zearalenone is another mycotoxin produced by Fusarium. It is similar in structure to the female sex hormone oestrogen and targets the reproductive organs.

Penicillium spp. Found in soil, food, cellulose, grains, paint, carpet, wallpaper, interior fiberglass duct insulation, and decaying vegetation, the Penicillium species can cause hypersensitivity, asthma, and allergic alveolitis.

The fungus Penicillium verrucosidin is a neurotoxin and affects the brain, and penicillic acid is another penicillium that causes kidney and liver damage. Penicillium infections are damaging to immunosuppressed individuals. Penicillium marneffei, for instance, is a fungus found in Southeast Asia that typically infects patients with AIDS. Spread through the air, it triggers a lung infection and then spreads to other areas of the body (lymphatic system, liver, spleen, and bones), and is often fatal. But not all penicillium mycotoxins are harmful – penicillin, the antibiotic, comes from the same family and has saved innumerable lives.

Watch out for Mycotoxins – the invisible spores

In certain conditions – and no one is quite sure what the precise triggers are – moulds produce mycotoxins, natural chemical poisons - and these are what cause your health issues. One mould species can create several different mycotoxins – and a variety of different moulds can produce identical mycotoxins – confusing! They can grow on crops and foods and usually flourish where it is warm and humid. They are known to interfere with RNA synthesis and may cause DNA damage. So even if you are not one of the 1 in 3 people who have a genetic susceptibility to mould, you may be one of the other two whose DNA is adversely affected.

Mycotoxins can be incredibly toxic to humans causing a variety of responses including cold/flu-like symptoms, sore throats, headaches, nose bleeds, fatigue, kidney and liver damage, diarrhoea, dermatitis, and immune suppression. Having said that, as already mentioned, penicillin is also a mycotoxin (Pencillium is the mould; Penicillin is it's poison; Brewer's Yeast is the mould – Alcohol is the poison) and the trichothecene mycotoxins are immune-stimulating at low doses, so not all mycotoxins are harmful.

Types of Toxic Mycotoxins

Aflatoxin. This mycotoxin is primarily produced by the Aspergillus species. It is one of the most potent carcinogens known to man and has been linked to a wide array of human health problems, including digestive problems, fertility issues and immunity suppression.

Ochratoxin. This mycotoxin is primarily produced by species of Penicillium (Penicillium verrucosum) and Aspergillus. It can be damaging to the kidneys / liver, and it is a suspected carcinogen. There is also evidence supporting its role in impairing immune system function.

Tricothecene. The toxin is produced by Stachybotrys spp. and Fusarium spp and has been flagged as a potential agent for use as a biological weapon. One of the more deadly mycotoxins, if it is ingested in large amounts it can severely damage the entire digestive tract and cause rapid death due to internal haemorrhaging. In low doses, however, it has been found to stimulate the immune system positively (Eduard, 2006).

Fumonisins – Produced by the genus Fusarium, this mould is often found in corn and maize and has been found to be carcinogenic.

Zearalenone – Produced by some Fusarium and Gibberella species of mould, this toxin is found in mouldy wheat and hay, and mimics oestrogen, affecting fertility and damaging the liver and kidneys.

7. MOULD IN YOUR HOME

Never underestimate how hard it is to get rid of mould, and don't put off dealing with it as soon as you spot it or smell it anywhere in your home.

50% of buildings in the USA are considered 'water damaged' – affected in some way by water infiltration, whether from the weather - rain and flooding - from damp, leaks in the pipes, trouble in the air conditioning or heating vents, or from condensation from poorly ventilated buildings with windows that are sealed shut at all times. Where there is water, mould will shortly afterwards always follow. Over 45 million people in the USA are estimated to live in 'mouldy' buildings and in the UK more than a third of houses are estimated to be contaminated with mould toxins. Not everyone living in a mould infested house will be affected by symptoms, but for those who are sensitive to the fungus, the effects can be seriously debilitating.

Make sure your house is healthy – with no damp basement or stagnant areas where the air doesn't flow. Condensation - on walls or windows, air-conditioning units, poor insulation and even metal window frames - can result in dampness, giving mould an opportunity to thrive.

It has been calculated that there are more than 1,000 different strains of moulds that exist inside the house. Fungi spread by releasing their spores into the air. They can multiply until there are thousands of spores in every cubic foot of air inside your house. These mould spores in turn release micro-toxins that float around in the atmosphere and flood the air that you breathe – invisibly, relentlessly and dangerously poisoning people who are susceptible to their toxins. They also grow on your furniture, on the walls or underneath the floorboards. The black mould that is often found behind your wallpaper or behind the bathroom tiles is also toxic.

Damp basements, airless spaces behind kitchen appliances and damp spots around window frames are all environments that encourage mould growth. It feeds on dry wall insulation, chipboard and plywood. Increased humidity in the air or in an unvented room multiplies its growth. Poorly maintained schools can become a breeding ground for moulds of all kinds, creating an environment that will infect its pupils and affect their learning capabilities and behaviours. The toxins from mould fungi spread through the air, and merely by breathing, you can become infected.

Do you work in a building with air conditioning? Air con units produce moisture on the cool surfaces of the systems, over which all the ventilation air you breathe in flows.[5] They can provide a breeding ground for mould and then rapidly and invisibly spread it through a building.[6]

---

[5] Bernstein et al 2006

[6] Ultraviolet germicidal irradiation of the wet surfaces of cooling coils and condensate drip pans in heating, ventilation and air conditioning systems substantially reduced symptoms amongst the occupants (Menzies et al 2003)

...at to do about it?

Find it!

Mould dims your energy. And it is unlikely that you will get better until your mould is dealt with. Do an inch by inch inspection of every room in your house – attic and basement included. Visible mould is easy to recognise – we have all seen those clumps of black clinging to the walls. There is usually some small physical sign of water damage – maybe only a tiny bubble on the wall indicating water penetration but track it down. If there is damp behind a wall, even a hot humid day can make the spore count go up dramatically. Most basements are likely to have problems. And make sure, if you can't see any traces, that you sniff conclusively. That wet sock, mildew smell is often a giveaway. And if you can't find anything at all at home – then double check your office, your children's schools, even your car, garden shed or boat. Rats can spread mould – and even a garden water sprinkler system, aimed at a wall by mistake, can be the source of much of your problem. www.moldcheck.com offers test strips that flag which rooms may be a mould hot spot. Dogs can also be trained to sniff out moulds. Become a detective – track it down!

Fix it!

Then, when you do find it, you need to deal with what caused the mould to grow in the first place. Was it a leak? Was it damp, condensation or poor ventilation?

Plaster check: Mould has to have a food to grow. Damp plasterboard is a favourite meal, and it can grow on both sides, so if you have a stud wall, it may well be living on the other side, just where you can't see it. Cut out a small section to check, and if it's bad news, you may well need to cut a bigger area out and re-plaster, or replace the wall altogether. On brick walls, or solid surfaces, you may just need to take the wallpaper off the affected area. Get the builders in and sort it. Paint the walls afterwards with Auro eco specialist anti-mould paint.

Then make an appointment with your doctor or naturopath to run blood or urine tests to find out how it's been affecting you too. Check inflammation levels, hormone disruption, antibody testing, and what is going on with your brain? If you are genetically susceptible to mould, you need to make sure you stay away from anywhere that is mouldy – other people's houses, shops, farm buildings. Cruise ships apparently have a big mould problem – so alter your holiday plans if you need to. Until you have rebuilt your immunity, even a breath in the wrong place can trigger a reaction.

Get mould experts in: Sometimes you just need the experts. Ask for personal recommendations and find a company who know exactly what to do. It is called mould remediation, and they will come round and do an inspection and take a mould history from you.

Check your air: The professionals will test the air that you have been breathing. They can supply you with machines that will suck out all the spore filled air: A photo catalytic oxidiser - PCO Unit – should do the trick. An air scrubber is a big fan with HEPA filters that purifies the air, effectively sucking up any dirty contaminated air and replacing it with pure air. It takes an hour or so to do. They can also check your bathrooms, remove any spore filled grout and install new and more powerful ventilation units. Buy your own air purifier to keep the air you breathe mould free.

Heat Treatment: Specialists can heat treat individual rooms, or indeed the whole house. This is the most effective anti-mould deterrent. Most moulds are destroyed at temperatures of 63 degrees C/145 degrees F for a period of 30 minutes.

Clean up the Contents: Your clothes need to be treated as well as the furniture and the carpets. If mould levels are really bad, you will need to replace your pillows, duvets, mattresses and keep any furniture slightly away from the walls so that the air can circulate. Otherwise, you may find mould multiplying on the back of your furniture.

A HEPA Vac will vacuum up all visible mould. This is a small vacuum cleaner with a very fine filter that captures the smallest particles and takes away the surface mould

A 'fogging' machine with biocide which emits a very fine spray into the air and settles, dissolving after an hour or so, is another option. You can't stay in the room whilst it happens – so not a very organic treatment, but sometimes toxic is the only way. ULV fogging or 'wet' fogging will remove any residual airborne contaminants.

Mould and Electro-magnetic Stress

Research has shown that electro-magnetic stress – the electrical frequencies given off by your phones, televisions sets, fridges, ovens and every electrical appliance that so much of our lives now depend on – can multiply mould growth.

Dr Klinghardt has experimented with mould cultures and found that they multiply dozens of times faster and release 600 times more toxins when they are also exposed to electromagnetic fields. Bin that microwave if you can! Clean up around the backs of your dishwashers and clothes dryers.

Natural ways to wipe out mould in your home

Tea Tree Oil: This is a controversial cure for mould in a room. Described as 'mould kryptonite' by some, others have no success with it at all. But worth experimenting with your particular type of mould. (Spray 2 teaspoons mixed in 2 cups of water and leave to dry)

Hydrogen Peroxide: this is an option that is anti-fungal, anti-bacterial and anti-viral. It smells fairly strong and works best on tiles and hard surfaces. Mix one teaspoon with one cup of water in a spray bottle and shake. Spray and let sit for 20 mins before wiping away.

Grapefruit seed extract: Destroys mould on walls and ceilings effectively. Put 10 drops in a cup of water into a spray bottle, shake well and spray directly onto the mouldy area you want to treat. Leave for 10 minutes and remove the debris, allowing the solution to dry naturally preventing any further mould growth.

Vinegar: Spray it, undiluted, onto any mouldy area and the research says you will destroy 82% of your problem.

MMS: There is a lot of controversy over Miracle Mineral Supplement, with all sorts of disinformation written up on the web. Please do your research and don't believe everything that you read. Follow the instructions precisely. I have used it for years and find it does just what its inventor claims for it – as long as you carefully follow the dosage directions.

To clear mould: Put 50 drops of activated MMS in a bowl in the middle of any room needing to be rid of mould. Close the doors and remove any pets. The CI02 gas (chlorine dioxide) will flood the room, neutralising germs and moulds in the air and in clothes and furniture. After two or so hours, the room should be free of the smell of damp.

You can also put 20 drops of MMS in a gallon of water (having activated it first in a glass as per the instructions and waited for three minutes before pouring it into the water) and put into a dehumidifier or diffuser. That will also neutralise the mould, but never be in or sleep in a room that has a dehumidifier full of MMS going.

Essential oil in a vaporiser: Experiment with 2 or 3 drops of Myrrh in a diffuser in a room. Myrrh is anti-microbial, anti-fungal and anti-inflammatory. It can also raise your body's resistance to mould. Fill a diffuser with Young Living's Thieves Oil which is a combination of clove, cinnamon, rosemary, eucalyptus, and lemon. It surrounds the mould and literally eats up the mould spores.

5 And the last case scenario: If your health is seriously affected by mould, then (dramatic though it sounds and however reluctant you are to do it) the only solution is to leave your home, and move house. Extreme, but then how valuable is your health? Be aware too that you need to heat treat all your possessions - your clothes, furniture, books - everything that you want to take with you. If you don't the mould will just travel along too…

8. MOULD IN YOUR BODY

Dr Richard Shoemaker, who has studied the effects of mould on thousands of patients, has concluded that fungal toxins cause chronic inflammation in the body, paralysing the body systems that would usually control it. The body's protective mechanisms stop working, and the immune system begins to fail. Fibromyalgia and chronic fatigue syndrome – those unexplained yet debilitating illnesses – may well have fungal toxicity at their root.

Things to consider:

1 Take a look in your mirror

Look in the mirror. Is your face, and your body, puffy and slightly swollen? Inflammation may be an indication that mould is at the heart of your problem. Do you eat meat? Do you love bread? Think carefully about how we produce our foods. We give the animals we eat antibiotics in their feed, and antibiotics are mycotoxins. Antibiotics are also growth promoters, intended to fatten up chickens, cows and lambs. And once they are fat, we eat them – along, unwittingly, with the mould we fed them on. We eat vast quantities of wheat too – much of which is also mouldy. Yeast makes bread rise – does it make us swell too? Are we making ourselves mouldy by mistake - and sick in the process?

2 Candida

Just for clarity – candida is not officially a mould, it's a yeast - but it is the trigger behind most fungal infections. Most of us have candida albicans to a certain degree, one of the most common, and trickiest, yeasts to eliminate from the body. It feeds on sugar and as sugar consumption has increased in recent decades, so has the growth of candida. Those cravings for a cup of hot tea and chocolate biscuits each day at 5pm? It's the candida in your gut crying out for food. Sugar addict? It's the candida you are carrying around inside you that yearns for the sweet stuff. The more it has spread throughout your body, the stronger your cravings are likely to be.

Have you been prescribed a course of anti-biotics recently and wiped out the gut bacteria that keeps your candida in check? Are you on the contraceptive pill; do you drink chlorinated water and eat daily doughnuts? You may well be being attacked by fungi on two sides – on the inside, as well as on the outside.

3 Consider the health issues linked to moulds

Jock itch? Toenail fungus? Vaginal yeast or ring worm? All indicate the presence of fungus in your body. Research papers have been written on the connections between cancer and mould, and diabetes and mould. Alzheimers, ADHD, autism, behavioural problems, as well as heart attacks, have all been linked to the effects of mycotoxins. Chronic fatigue, fibromyalgia and Lyme's disease have been shown to have a connection to mould too. Brain fog, depression, joint pain, pneumonia, weight gain, sinus infection, sore throats: the lists goes on and on. The more exposure you have to mould, and for the longer the period of time, the more it affects your hormones, your DNA and your brain.

'Mould can cause chronic illnesses that 'masquerade' as other diseases..' according to Mark Hyman, Chairman of the Institute for Functional Medicine. Dr. Elizabeth Moore Landaker has gone on record as saying, 'All fungi make triglycerides and many fungi make sterols, the second half of the word cholesterol.' Perhaps high cholesterol levels are more to do with mould triggered inflammation than anything else? Fungal toxins clog arteries, so mycotoxins may be a principal trigger for atherosclerosis linked heart issues, not fat as is often suggested. Statins used to be called 'anti-fungals' long ago, and were given out for exactly that problem. Now they are used for the heart, 'lowering' cholesterol and triglyceride levels. Yet perhaps those numbers fall principally because the statins are destroying any fungus present in the bloodstream?

4 Mould and your brain

It is never normal to have brain symptoms. Loss of memory at whatever age – 40, 50 or 70 – is not normal, or 'just a sign of getting older' - but a sign of something wrong.

Mould can swing your moods and switch your brain into a state of rage, anger or irritation. It can affect the basal ganglia of the brain, which deals with how joyful and how driven a person is. It can overwhelm you with sadness and depression and affect the clarity of your thinking. Whichever area of your brain it gets into – and remember that merely breathing mouldy air in through your nose can directly access the inner part of your brain – it attacks and affects. Mould is poisonous to brain cells. It loves damp and warmth, so the vitreous liquid in the eye is another perfect place for it to lodge. Clear up any mould there and your eyesight may well improve.

Have your organisational skills got less precise and are you losing the ability to learn from your mistakes? Are you losing your memory and finding it hard to learn new things? It could be mould. Your frontal lobe deals with judgement, forethought and impulse control. It may have accessed your temporal lobes.

Frequently angry when you didn't use to be? It may have affected your Amygdala, the almond shaped area behind your eyes. Mould can shrink your pituitary and damage your thyroid too. How much it affects you is down to the strength of your immune system. But never despair – it is entirely possible to sort the issues and get your brain and your physical health back– just as long as you identify the problem. Check your life for the extent mould may be affecting your health.

5 Mould and Sleep

Mould has been shown to affect sleep patterns and interrupt circadian rhythms. If you don't get seven hours sleep a night, 700 health promoting genes switch off, lowering your immunity and leaving you open to myriad problems. Both nightmares and sleepwalking are said to be connected to the presence of mould.

Natural Anti-mould Remedies to Reboot Your Body

Experiment with the following and find which one works for you:
Sign up for a therapy session: Health Kinesiology; NAET and Field Control Therapy are all ways of identifying whether you are affected by a specific mould, and offer methods of strengthening your immune system and upping your natural defences.

Oxygen therapy can lift the fog. If you have a Hyperbaric oxygen chamber anywhere in your area, sign up for a few sessions and bring your mind back to life. Research shows it takes around 20 sessions to clear the fungus.

Far Infra-red saunas – these heat your body from the inside first, and regular sessions can destroy the mould. Ozone saunas also kill mould – and because they open your pores as you sweat, can penetrate deep into your body to root out the toxins. Do a sauna daily if you can.

Glutathione – Glutathione is your body's most powerful antioxidant and strengthens your liver function. You can buy it in liposomal form and take it daily (300 msgs twice a day), or for an added boost, sign up for an intravenous drip.

Take activated charcoal – This binds to the mycotoxins which are poisoning you and creating inflammation throughout your body, though again allow several months to clear the symptoms. Dave Asprey from Bulletproof claims to provide the finest activated charcoal particles and he also recommends using Alieve liquid gel capsules alongside – one or two a week – which he says will bind to your bile, allowing the body to excrete any mould. Use alongside glutathione, but he recommends always having a two hour gap between taking the two of them. Myrrhinil Intest, an anti-fungal, absorbs the toxins via medically activated carbon and also strengthens the immune system.

Supplement with natural anti-inflammatories to restore lost energy and stop sore joints and muscles – Boswellia, Holy Basil, Turmeric and Green tea.

Curcumin: Take liposomal curcumin two to three times daily to reduce the inflammation caused by mould sensitivity.

Artichoke leaf extract – A study published in the Journal of Agricultural Food Chemistry in 2004 found that extract of artichoke leaf successfully destroyed moulds and yeasts.

Vitamin D – Make sure your Vitamin D Levels are high, which should reduce the effects of mould allergies.

Phosphatidyl Choline: – preferably in liposomal form – will strengthen any neurological damage caused by mould and boost any blood brain barrier damaged by mould mycotoxins.

Colloidal silver: Google victuruslibertas.com to see a short video showing colloidal silver wiping out mould. Colloidal silver will also boost your immune system; buy it in spray form and follow the instructions on the bottle. Certain health clinics also offer intravenous silver which efficiently removes fungi, bacteria and viruses from your system.

Liquid Chlorophyll: Chlorophyll is the bright green substance that gives plants their colour, helping them turn sunlight into energy via photosynthesis. As a supplement, it is anti-inflammatory and has been shown to be effective in reducing candida and other fungi levels in the body, keeping their numbers in check because of its anti-microbial properties.

EDTA nasal sprays: Living in a mouldy house can give you a severe case of sinusitis. Clear your nasal passages by investing in an EDTA spray which destroys the biofilm colonised by the myctotoxins. Another option is BEG, which combines three medications in one bottle – bactroban (mupirocin), EDTA and gentamicin. Together they combine to attack and dissolve the biofilm in which the mould and bacteria live. BEG also wipes out MARCoNS (Multiple Antibiotic Resistant Coagulase Negative Staphylococci) which are also found in the nose and are a sign of mould infestation. BEG-1 contains the antifungal itraconazole, and BEG-V the antifungal voriconazole.

MSH nasal spray – increase your levels of melanocyte stimulating hormone (MSH) which stops inflammation. Melanotan is a European brand.

Liposomal DIM: Mould interferes with the ability of our cells to detoxify, interrupting the Nrf2 defense mechanism. Take two squirts twice a day.

Homeopathy: HMV and Bio-Allers are two homeopathic preparations made from moulds that will reduce the effects the spores have.

Essential Oils: Experiment with Thyme, Clove, Sage and Cinnamon essential oils, each of which is reported to counteract mould growth and see which works for you. Consult a specialist for correct dosage and how to take them.

Vitamin C: kills fungus, rapidly. Take liposomal vitamin C orally every day, or sign up for a series of Vitamin C IV's. Enemas using vitamin C have also been reported to dramatically lower the body's mould load. Always check dosage with your doctor or natural health adviser. Make sure you use Ascorbic Acid not Ester-C and find a brand which is corn-free as many companies make vitamin C using a technique of fermenting mould with GMO corn on an industrial scale. 'It is manufactured using a mould that feeds on corn syrup glucose'.

Caprylic Acid: Caprylic acid is a saturated fatty acid that comes from coconut oil and essentially makes tiny holes in the cell walls of any invading yeast, killing them in the process.

Chlorella taken in high doses will bind to any mould toxins, allowing your body to excrete them slowly and safely. Take 20 of the tiny tablets 3 times a day before meals.

Liposomal Alpha Lipoic Acid (ALA) strengthens the liver and is a powerful anti-oxidant, helping the body to recover from mould spore attack and to more effectively get rid of any invading mould toxins.

Top Tip: Citrisafe Products – check out www.citrisafe.com for a range of natural mould and mildew removal products, both for your body and your home.

Home Biotic – www.homebiotic.com – is an all-natural probiotic spray for your home filled with bacteria that eats mould. One application covers 90m2 and lasts for approximately 6 months.

There are also pharmaceutical solutions that work:

Fluconazole (Diflucan) reduces mould and yeast levels inside the body. You can do a gentle 60-day course, or a more intense week-long course. Be careful with the recommended dosage, however, because too much of it can cause liver damage. Always consult your doctor for a prescription.

Glitazones – The drugs Actos and Avandia are older type blood sugar lowering drugs that reduce inflammation and insulin resistance. They are used as diabetes medications primarily but an Indian research paper reported that they show 'remarkable' antifungal properties, and a Tennessee study reported them as comparable to Diflucan (Fluconazole) in their ability to stop fungal growth.

Olmesartan (Olmetec) was developed as a high blood pressure treatment, but has been shown to reduce mould levels in studies. It activates Vitamin D receptors (VDR), blocks the production of NFkB and reduces inflammation.

Cholestyramine (CSM): is an FDA-approved medication that has been used for more than 40 years now in the treatment of high cholesterol levels and it has also been shown to successfully treat mould related illnesses safely and in a short period of time.

Cholestyramine (not taken with food) is not absorbed but binds to mould toxins in your gut allowing the body to excrete it harmlessly in the stool. The FDA approved dose is either 9 grams of CSM, or 4 grams of Questran Light (note this product contains aspartame), taken 4 times a day. Side effects may include heartburn (which can be minimised by mixing the CSM in apple juice or cranberry juice), reflux and bloating. Constipation is another possible problem, so it is recommended to drink several litres of water daily whilst on the protocol, or add a quarter teaspoon of magnesium citrate which eliminates constipation issues. Taking psyllium with cholestyramine also reduces most side effects.

CSM Protocol
1. On an empty stomach, take one scoop of CSM (9 grams), mix with water, or juice, 4-6 oz. Stir well and swallow.
2. Follow up with a large glass of 4-6 oz of water.
3. After 30 minutes, you may eat or take any medications (wait at least 2 hours before taking thyroxine, digitalis, theophylline, Coumadin; always

check with your doctor).
4. Take CSM 4 times a day.
5. Always wait at least 60 minutes after eating before taking your next CSM dose.
6. Use acid blocking medications as needed

Mould Don'ts:

Don't use antibiotics unless you really need to: Antibiotics are made of toxic moulds like aspergillus and penicillium

Don't use metal colonoscopy tubes – Be careful when you go in for the process. Hospitals used to use replaceable plastic tubing, but nowadays, perhaps for budgetary reasons, they are often metal, and despite sterilisation, mycotoxins have been shown to survive, possibly passing via the tubes to the next patient. Make sure that patient isn't you!

Don't use pesticides in your garden: Some chemicals and pesticides use toxic moulds that produce T-2 mycotoxins (Trichothecenes) - Agent Orange and RoundUp included.

9. MOULD IN THE FOODS YOU EAT

Think about a lovely piece of French cheese – or that Christmas Stilton. Have you considered that the striking blue lines are real life bacteria? That you are feeding your body with mould? Do you still pop that last slice of bread in the toaster, mouldy splodges or not? After all, it's only penicillin – must be good for you?

Actually it's not.

Remember the Middle Ages, when mouldy bread was one of the major risks of death, up there with the Plague? Mould in your food puts mould in your body. Do you open the fridge door and throw out the food that has been sitting there for far too long often enough? Have you noticed the fine mist of grey mould that rises from the plastic bag as you throw out last months' lemons? Get cleaning the cracks and crannies of your refrigerator, and most of all get rid of all food that isn't fresh.

It takes time to reduce your body's 'mould load'. Mould makes you sensitive to certain foods, bloating your body, dulling your mind and leaving you tired and aching. Commit to three weeks of eating fresh food only. Cut out dairy and wheat because mould makes you gluten and casein intolerant.

Keep a food diary and see if you can chart a difference.

Drink a daily green juice of cucumber and celery to alkalize your body because mould cannot thrive in an alkaline environment. Add in a whole clove of garlic (garlic detoxifies and stimulates your immune system, and works against fungus, bacteria and viruses), a chunk of ginger (which is also anti-fungal and anti-bacterial) and some flakes of cayenne pepper.

Take a daily probiotic, the good bacteria will control the 'bad' bacteria in your gut. And drink a morning cup of anti-mould apple cider vinegar in warm water which will help you de-bloat.

Cut out mould's favourite foods altogether and replace them with an overload of fresh vegetables and whole foods and you will give your body a chance to repair and revive.

Mould Loves:

All sugars and all carbohydrates – pasta, cakes, biscuits
Alcohol – beer, gin, whisky, cider and wine
Mushrooms – steer clear of moulds fungi friends
Grains – wheat, barley and rye.
Rice – Aflatoxin is found in rice. Cooking only destroys around 50% of the mould – even in a pressure cooker that figure only increases to 70% - and none of the poisons from the mycotoxins which you then eat[7]
Hard cheeses - which are made with a fungal ingredient
Bread - because the flour it is made from often sits for months in damp conditions and breeds mould. Mouldy grains crash your blood sugar levels and damage your pancreas. Cut them out entirely if you can.
Coffee – most coffee beans are mouldy by the time they are ground. Bulletproof coffee is said by Dave Asprey, its founder, to be the only mould free brand.
Peanuts – A 1993 study identified 24 different types of fungi on the outside of a single peanut sample – and these peanuts had already been sterilized. One of the mycotoxins found on peanuts is aflatoxin , which can cause cancer.
Sweetcorn and corn on the cob – those yellow green spots on your corn on the cob are the aflatoxin mycotoxin. Highly toxic and behind many health issues. Careful of readymade cinema and supermarket popcorn.
Teabags – bet you never thought about the mould that grows on the bags after months of being stored in damp warehouses? Keep your loose leaf tea in an airtight container or the same thing happens. Damp kitchen, moisture in the air and that's where the mould will grow.

Mould Hates:

Garlic: Eat it raw and whole if you can – or add to your daily green juice in liquidized form. Garlic is anti-fungal, anti-bacterial and anti-viral.
Ginger: Add it to your daily juice – it is also anti-fungal and anti-bacterial.
Cayenne Pepper: which magnifies the effects of other anti-fungals
Goldenseal: Also anti-bacterial.

---

[7] Coomes, T.J., Crowther, P.C., Feuell, A.J. & Francis, B.J., Experimental detoxification of groundnut meals containing aflatoxin, Nature, 290, 1966, 406

10. REFERENCES

'Mould, Mildew and Fungus. Mould and its poisonous by-products'
Doug Kaufman

'Fungal Bionics – Hope at Last'
Dr Kostantini

'Secret Enemies - The Mould Toxin Illness'
Roland Brandmaier MD

BEGINNER'S GUIDE TO TOXIC MOLD:
http://paradigmchange.me/beginners/

SURVIVINGMOLD.COM:
http://www.survivingmold.com/

MOLD DIAGNOSIS:
http://www.survivingmold.com/diagnosis

MOLD TREATMENT:
http://www.survivingmold.com/treatment

PARADIGM CHANGE:
http://paradigmchange.me/

BIOTOXIN ILLNESS TEST
http://biotoxinjourney.com/biotoxinillnesstest/

MOLDY COMMUNITY RESOURCES:
http://paradigmchange.me/mold-blogs/

www.bulletproofexec.com
Watch mycotoxin video on youtube v=mj887HK621E

ABOUT THE AUTHOR

Sara Davenport is 56 years old, married, with two daughters. She lives in London, England and is passionate about showing people how to get healthy and stay healthy. She graduated from Cambridge University where she studied History of Art and opened the first gallery in the world specialising in 19th century dog paintings. She sold it at auction in 1997 to raise the funds to set up what is now one of the UK's leading breast cancer charities - Breast Cancer Haven. The charity has 6 centres across the UK and offers advice, counselling and complementary therapies to anyone affected by breast cancer, free of charge.

She writes a weekly blog, RebootHealth.co.uk, which looks at all aspects of health and healing, bringing you a regular dose of DIY get-well advice. From nutrition to detox, sleep to air pollution and the best health tests on the market, ReBoot Health covers a wide range of topics, delivering the low down on conventional medicine and complementary therapies.

'Reboot Your Health: Simple DIY Tests and Solutions to Assess and Improve Your Health' is her first published book. It helps you to find your own unique 'Health Baseline' - establishing what is working in your body and what is not - and then showing you how to sort any issues, simply, inexpensively and naturally. If you want to live long and happy into your older age, make this a health essential!

Printed in Great Britain
by Amazon